Celtic Gods and Heroes

John Green

DOVER PUBLICATIONS, INC.
Mineola, New York

Copyright

Copyright © 2003 by Dover Publications, Inc.
All rights reserved.

Bibliographical Note

Celtic Gods and Heroes is a new work, first published by Dover Publications, Inc., in 2003.

DOVER *Pictorial Archive* SERIES

This book belongs to the Dover Pictorial Archive Series. You may use the designs and illustrations for graphics and crafts applications, free and without special permission, provided that you include no more than four in the same publication or project. (For permission for additional use, please write to Permissions Department, Dover Publications, Inc., 31 East 2nd Street, Mineola, N.Y. 11501.)

However, republication or reproduction of any illustration by any other graphic service, whether it be in a book or in any other design resource, is strictly prohibited.

Library of Congress Cataloging-in-Publication Data

Green, John, 1958-
  Celtic gods and heroes / John Green.
    p. cm— (Dover pictorial archive series)
  ISBN 0-486-42792-7 (pbk.)
    1. Gods, Celtic—Pictorial works. 2. Mythology, Celtic—Pictorial works. 3. Heroes—Mythology—British Isles—Pictorial works. I. Title. II. Series.

BL900.G72 2003
299'.16—dc21

                    2003046167

Manufactured in the United States of America
Dover Publications, Inc., 31 East 2nd Street, Mineola, N.Y. 11501

Note

In modern times, the term "Celtic" evokes a wide range of imagery and emotion, having profound significance for spiritualists and sports enthusiasts alike. The history of this ancient people has become shrouded in myth and legend, but certain key facts are known. As the dominant inhabitants of the European continent, British Isles, and parts of Asia Minor during the fifth and fourth centuries B.C., the Celts were universally feared as a group of barbarous warmongers. The Celts were not a single race of people, but were comprised of many clans scattered throughout these regions, sharing a common lifestyle rather than a biological bond. In the few centuries before the birth of Christ, the Romans systematically invaded and annexed the vast majority of Celtic-occupied land, largely suppressing the foreign lifestyles and beliefs, and absorbing some elements into their own. Though the Celtic culture enjoyed a renaissance in early medieval Britain after the collapse of the Roman Empire, details of its true origins have faded over time.

Since the pre-Romantic Celts left relatively few writings and artifacts to reveal and preserve their history, most of our modern knowledge derives from early Greek and Roman written observations, and from sixth and seventh centuries A.D. transcriptions of Celtic stories by Christian monks in Ireland. However, these records, though useful, are undoubtedly corrupted by human error, prejudice, and the passage of time. At best, contemporary historians can piece together a vague but nevertheless fascinating portrait of the early Celts.

It is due to the remarkable efforts by the ancient scribes and the continued preservation of manuscripts that we are able to enjoy these wonderful stories. The legends often seem like Celtic knotwork, with heroes moving from one tale to another, driven by passion, sorrow, love, jealousy, hate, vengeance, and courage—all woven together to provide an intriguing glimpse into the Celtic world, as well as human nature.

Note: Some names and places are spelled differently among the various reference sources consulted. Generally, the most commonly used spelling was selected for this text.

Tuatha Dé Danann

Early legends deal with the Tuatha Dé Danann (which means "tribes of the goddess Dana"), a race of divine beings who came to Ireland on an enchanted cloud, bearing magical skills. They also brought four talismans: the Stone of Fál, which screamed when the rightful king of Ireland placed his foot upon it; the Spear of Lugh, which ensured victory; the magic Sword of Nuada, a weapon that killed with one blow; and the Cauldron of the Dagda, which quenched every appetite

Legend tells of the battle between the Tuatha Dé Danann and the land's then-occupants, the Firbolgs. Using magic, the Dananns were victorious in winning the territory, but nevertheless granted the Firbolgs a province in Ireland of their own called Connacht. Since the Danann's King Nuada had lost his hand in the battle, disqualifying him from ruling, a man named Bres was chosen to be the new king of Ireland. However, Bres proved to be a stingy and inhospitable monarch, and was swiftly replaced by the magically healed Nuada. In revenge, Bres then called upon Balor, the king of the Fomorians, a violent race of misshapen brutes. Balor and the Fomorians easily conquered and oppressed the people of Ireland, including the Tuatha Dé Danann and Firbolgs. In time, the hero Lugh, the Sun-god and grandson of Balor, managed to slay his grandfather and drive out the Fomorians, thus winning the crown of Ireland.

The Tuatha Dé Danann ruled Ireland until their defeat by the Milesians, after which they withdrew underground beneath grass mounds to live, without fear of discovery, in subterranean palaces glittering with magical wonders.

fomorians

The Fomorians were cruel, monstrous savages representing the dark forces and the powers of evil. In Irish mythology, the Fomorians rose from the sea to challenge the then-rulers of Ireland, the Firbolgs and Tuatha Dé Danann. They ruthlessly demanded exorbitant tributes (forced payments) from their defeated opponents, seizing food, stock, and even children. Their stronghold was said to be on Tory Island off the coast of Donegal, an island of precipices and wild cliffs rising from the depths of the Atlantic.

The most feared of the Fomorians was Balor, a king of mighty stature with an "evil eye" that could kill enemies with one deadly glance—making him nearly invincible. Early on, Balor had been told in a druidic prophecy that he would be slain by his own grandson. To prevent this, he imprisoned his only child, a daughter named Ethlinn, in a high tower on the remote headland of Tor Mor off Tory Island. After Ethlinn was grown, Balor happened to steal a magical cow from Kian, the son of the god Dian Cecht. Seeking revenge, Kian sought the advice of a Druidess, who guided him to Ethlinn. In time, Ethlinn gave birth to three boys. Enraged, Balor commanded the infants to be drowned. One, however, survived—Lugh, the Sun-god.

Lugh grew into brave, intelligent youth with superior fighting skills and a magical sword that slew at one blow. The Dananns recognized his potential as their liberator, and quickly made him their leader in the final revolt against the Fomorians. Armed with a slingshot, Lugh waited until the eye of Balor momentarily closed from fatigue, then shot a stone into the Fomorian's head, killing him instantly. After the death of their leader, the vicious Fomorians were soon driven out and the people of Ireland were free once again.

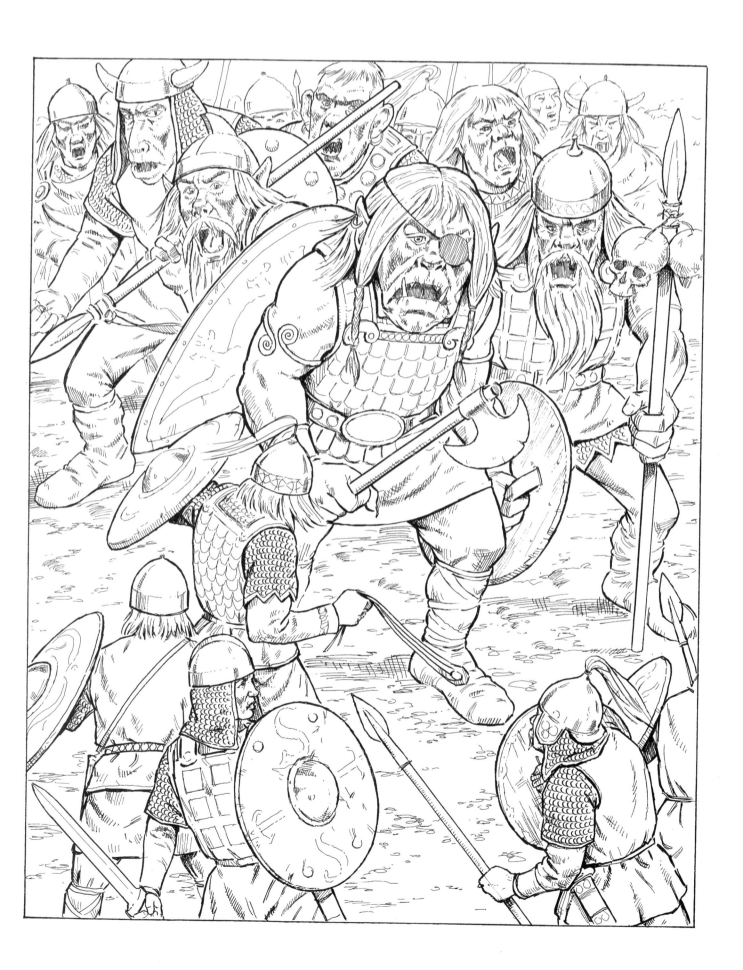

The Dagda

The Dagda, or "The Good God," was the revered chieftain and supreme leader of the Tuatha Dé Danann. He acquired his name because he excelled in everything, especially magic, warfare, and craftsmanship. In some stories, he is seen as the father of Angus, the Irish god of love, and the popular goddess Brigit, among others. The Dagda was reputed to have a club so enormous that eight men were needed to carry it. This weapon was imbued with magical powers, with one end capable of killing nine men at once, and the other able to restore life to the dead.

Like all the Tuatha Dé Danann, the Dagda was a master of music. He owned an enchanted harp that could fly through the air at his call and compel its listeners to cry, laugh, or weep, depending on the music played on its strings. The Dagda was also associated with abundance, as he possessed a cauldron that could satisfy the hunger of any number of people.

The Dagda's own appetite for food almost matched his cauldron's ability to quench it. One legend tells of the Dagda visiting the Fomorians during a truce. At mealtime, the Danann king was led to a gigantic pit filled with porridge, milk, flour, and fat, as well as whole pigs, sheep, and goats. He was ordered to eat everything in the pit or be put to death. With a ladle big enough to seat two men, the Dagda shocked the Fomorians by consuming the entire lot, even scraping up the dregs and gravel at the bottom of the pit with his finger to complete his meal.

Ogma

gma, a son of the Dagda, was Ireland's god of literature and eloquence, and was nicknamed Cermait, or "Honey-Mouthed." He is credited with inventing Ogham, one of the earliest systems of writing, which used a series of vertical or sloping lines inscribed on a base line to portray letters. The sagas tell of vast libraries of Ogham writing, though only a few carved stones have survived. Ogma was renowned as a great poet, orator, and—as the champion of the Tuatha Dé Danann—a fierce warrior as well.

During a battle with the Fomorians, Ogma slew Indech, the son of the Fomorian goddess and leader, Domnu. After the terrible struggle, the triumphant Ogma claimed as a prize a Fomorian sword that was capable of recounting all the deeds it had performed.

In some Irish myths, Ogma is said to convey the souls of the dead to the "other world," a wonderful and peaceful place where souls could rest prior to their rebirth.

Brigit

Brigit (or Brigid) was known in Irish mythology as the goddess of prosperity, childbirth, and healing. She was the daughter of the Dagda and the Morrigan, a war-goddess who was also known as the Phantom Queen. Brigit would also occasionally be known as Dana, from which the Tuatha Dé Danann ("tribes of the goddess Dana") derived their name.

Brigit was a goddess held in high honor by the pagan Celts, particularly in Ireland. As a celebration of the season of renewal, a festival known as "Imbolg" was held in her name each year in early February. When Christianity reached Ireland in the fifth century, its teachings dismissed the mythical races revered by the pagans, but some aspects of these beliefs were incorporated into the church. As beloved as she was, Brigit was not easily discarded, and many historians believe she was soon appropriated by Christianity to become Saint Brigid of Ireland, still honored to this day.

Bran mac Febal

Bran mac Febal, an Irish king, was the hero of the most famous of the Celtic voyage myths. His great odyssey began one day at his fortress, when he was lulled to sleep by sweet, mysterious music. Shortly afterward, a woman appeared before Bran and his company as if from nowhere, though her beauty, dress, and magical entrance left no doubt that she was of divine race. Turning towards Bran, she began to sing, extolling the wonders and delights of a host of paradise-like islands to the west, inviting Bran to visit. When her song was finished, she vanished from sight.

The next day, Bran sailed westward with twenty-seven kinsmen. Their first encounter was with the sea god, Manannan mac Lir, who rode on the waters in a magical chariot. He, too, sang of the wonders that awaited them, especially at the Isle of Women. When they reached the island, the leader of the women called to Bran to come ashore, but Bran was hesitant. She threw a ball of thread at him that stuck to Bran's hand and, as if by magic, drew the boat ashore. Once on land, Bran and his men enjoyed the delicious food, comfortable beds, and enchanting company. They quickly forgot about Ireland and lived a life of pleasure and indulgence for a year, after which one of the men grew homesick and persuaded Bran to return home. The leader of the women warned Bran that he would not be able to set foot in Ireland again, but the sailors nevertheless set off on the journey east.

Upon reaching the shore of his homeland, Bran called out to the large group of people that had gathered there. Remembering the warning, he identified himself and soon discovered that nobody recognized him, though they remembered his name as that of a legendary hero who had embarked on a great voyage hundreds of years ago. At this, the homesick crew member leapt ashore, only to be turned into a pile of ash when his feet touched the earth. Bran then told his story to the crowd of people and, without any other recourse, sadly set sail once more, never to return to his beloved Ireland again.

Manannan mac Lir

Manannan mac Lir is one of the most popular gods in Irish mythology. He was lord of the sea just as his father, Lir, had been. He was protector of Ireland, and it was said that anyone approaching the island with the intent to conquer it would hear the fearsome stomping of his feet and thunderous flapping of his cloak at night. The Isle of Man, off the coast of Ireland, was said to be his throne.

Manannan mac Lir appears in many of the Irish legends. As ruler of the sea, which contained the Islands of the Dead, he was one of several supposed guides to the afterlife. A master of the magical arts with the ability to change shape, Manannan also possessed many wonderful treasures, including a sword named Fragarach ("The Answerer") that sliced through the strongest armor, and a cloak that could take on every color, just like the sea. He had a boat called *Ocean Sweeper*, which needed no oars or sail because it was powered by the thoughts of its commander. Manannan's steed, a white horse named Aonbarr, was able to walk on both land and water.

According to some legends, Manannan mac Lir granted the Tuatha Dé Danann the power of invisibility after they were defeated by the Milesians. He then brought them to secret underground retreats, where they could live in peace and prosperity.

Branwen

Branwen, the sister of Brân the Blessed, a great warrior king of Britain, was one of the three chief ladies of the land and widely admired for her beauty. Her tragic tale is well known in Celtic mythology. In it, King Matholaw of Ireland asked Brân for his sister's hand in marriage, in order that the two kingdoms could be joined and benefit from united strength. Brân agreed, and the wedding took place at Aberffraw, where large tents had to be erected to comfortably accommodate the Brân's giant stature. However, Evnissyen, another of Branwen's brothers, was bitter at not being consulted about the marriage. He mutilated King Matholaw's horses, deeply insulting the proud monarch with this unprovoked attack. To make amends, Brân showered King Matholaw with gifts, including new horses and a magic cauldron that could rejuvenate the dead. Unfortunately, King Matholaw's subjects never forgot the terrible insult to their king, and Branwen was soon forced to work in the castle kitchens and endure cruel beatings daily.

Desperate to escape such ill treatment, Branwen cared for a young starling and trained it to find her brother. Carrying a letter, it flew to Britain, finding Brân and delivering the sad message. Brân immediately prepared a huge invasion fleet and destroyed King Matholaw's army, though the magic cauldron turned out to be an ironic and regrettable gift. In the end, Brân was mortally wounded by a poisoned arrow and commanded his few remaining men to sever his head and bury it in Britain, pointing his face towards the sea to ward off any invaders. Broken-hearted at the many deaths she had caused, Branwen soon afterward died of grief and remorse.

Cathbad the Druid

athbad was seer and druid to Ulster's King Conchobar mac Nessa. In Celtic society, druids were a pervasive influence; as intellectuals, they brought order to a society of warriors, and as priests, they served as the sole intermediary between man and god. Druids were extensive scholars, sometimes spending as many as twenty years studying and memorizing such orally shared knowledge as ceremonial procedures, spells, history, genealogy, healing arts, law, and philosophy. Exempt from military service and taxes, the druid's privileged and respected position was greatly sought after by young men.

Cathbad the Druid appears in many of the legends, foretelling events and casting mystical spells. His prophesies were many and included the prediction of his grandson Cuchulainn's glorious but short life, and the destruction that the maiden Deirdre's wondrous beauty would bring to Ulster.

Deirdre, though much younger than Conchobar, had been promised to him when she came of age, in order to thwart Cathbad's prediction at her birth. Shortly before her marriage, however, one of Conchobar's noblemen became enthralled by her beauty and agreed to her pleas to rescue her from the aging king. A few years later, Conchobar pretended to forgive the errant couple and had them escorted back to his kingdom, where he promptly threatened their lives. As they tried to escape, Cathbad agreed to help the king, as long as they would be unharmed, by conjuring a lake of slime to hinder their flight. Betraying his word, Conchobar had the nobleman and his brothers killed, causing the grief-stricken Deirdre to commit suicide shortly afterward. As punishment for his treachery, Cathbad cursed Conchobar, vowing that none of his descendants would ever rule Emain Macha, the capital of Ulster, ever again.

Queen Medb

Medb, the "Warrior Queen of Connacht," was a haughty and willful leader—a classic example of the fierce and cunning female that appears often in Celtic myth. Medb (pronounced "Maev") and her husband, King Ailill, ruled Connacht and kept its formidable army in active warfare—usually against Ulster—marking her reign with much bloodshed and sorrow.

It was Medb who, in her greed and pride, initiated the devastating Cattle-Raid of Cualgne, in which countless men were killed on both the Connacht and Ulster sides. One day, Medb and Ailill idly began tallying up their respective riches to determine who had more wealth. They proved to be nearly equal, except that Ailill possessed the marvelous White-Horned Bull, which was descended from the fairies. To even the score, Medb asked Daire of Ulster for his similarly exceptional animal, the Brown Bull of Cualgne. Although initially willing to lend the bull to Medb, Daire overheard Medb's messenger bragging that the queen could easily take the Brown Bull by force if Daire didn't agree to her request. In a temper, Daire refused to part with the Bull, and Medb furiously gathered her army to fulfill her messenger's boast. And so the tragic and ruinous Cattle-Raid of Cualgne was begun.

After the death of her husband, Medb retired to an island on Loch Ryve, where she made a habit of bathing every morning in a pool. Forbay, son of Conchobar mac Nessa, stalked the queen and found her retreat. Observing her daily ritual, he carefully measured the distance between the pool and the shore, and practiced with a sling-shot until he was able to knock an apple from the top of a pole at the same distance. He stealthily made his way back to the pool and skillfully shot Medb between the eyes with a stone, ending the hateful career of Connacht's mightiest warrior queen.

Cuchulainn

Cuchulainn was a valiant champion of Ireland and celebrated hero of Celtic legend, whose exploits rivaled those of Achilles and Hercules from Greek and Roman myth. He was born to the god Lugh and Dechtire, the daughter of Cathbad the Druid. Though he was originally called Setanta, he acquired his new name because he killed a fierce dog belonging to Culann, the smith. To compensate for the loss of the great protector of Culann's home and flocks, Setanta vowed to guard them himself until a new dog could be raised and trained. From that day on, he was known as Cuchulainn, the "Hound of Culann."

Cuchulainn became a great warrior, able to transform himself into a terrifying figure when pressed by his enemies. His body would shake, his muscles shift, his face distort, and his heart would beat with the roar of a lion. Foam would gush from his mouth and a blinding light and sparks of fire would blaze from his head. His four-colored hair would tangle into a bush and a great jet of blood would shoot from his scalp until it blotted out the daylight with its gloom.

In the epic tale of the Cattle-Raid of Cualgne, Cuchulainn plays a critical role in the mighty war between Ulster and Connacht. The hero fought and won every battle until Ulster was finally victorious. However, the relatives of Cuchulainn's victims banded together to seek revenge and bewitched him to believe there was a great battle being fought outside of his fortress. Longing to join the fight, Cuchulainn was restrained by his friends, but soon heard a voice calling that his home and all of Ulster was destroyed. Ignoring his friends' protests, he seized his weapons and ran outside. Through trickery and magic, Cuchulainn was weakened and forced to surrender three magic spears that were destined to slay kings. One killed his master charioteer. Another struck down his matchless horse, Gray of Macha. The last was flung into Cuchulainn himself. Wounded, the hero staggered to a pillar and bound himself to it so that he would die standing upright. The jubilant Connacht soldiers cut off his head as a prize, ending the brief but brilliant life of the legendary hero of Ulster.

Conall

Conall the Victorious was a vassal of King Conchobar and brother in arms to Cuchulainn. The two had sworn if either was killed first, the other would avenge him. As one of Ulster's respected champions, Conall appears in many of the legends as an able and courageous warrior.

Soon after Cuchulainn was killed and his enemies en route to bring his head to Queen Medb of Connacht, Conall arrived and raced off in pursuit. Reaching the soldiers, he killed them all, one by one, in revenge for the death of Cuchulainn. Conall retrieved the hero's head, which split the stone on which it was placed with the force of its posthumous power and buried itself into the slab. He then brought the stone to Cuchulainn's wife, along with a long string of the heads of the Connacht soldiers that he had slain. Thus, Conall had fulfilled his promise to avenge Cuchulainn's death.

In a later story, the warriors of Ulster and Connacht were assembled in Leinster to lay claim to their host's magnificent dog, which was faster than any animal in Ireland. As they feasted together, they debated who should have the honor of carving the roast boar. It was agreed that the greatest warrior should have the privilege, and Ket, the champion of Connacht, appeared to be winning the game. At the last moment, Conall strode into the hall and demanded that Ket step down from the table. When Ket challenged him, saying that his brother Anluan could easily beat the Ulster champion, Conall responded by reaching under his clothes and flinging Anluan's severed head at Ket's feet. In a frenzy, the men from both kingdoms jumped from their chairs and—drawing their swords—leapt at each other's throats. In the midst of the fighting, the esteemed dog was unfortunately killed and the warriors had to return home empty-handed.

Cernunnos

ernunnos, the god of life, death, and rebirth, was worshipped throughout the Celtic world for his power over men. Images of this deity are frequently found on Celtic artifacts all over Europe, including the famous Gundestrup cauldron, one of the most important surviving pieces dating from that era.

Cernunnos, the "Horned One," was typically depicted with deer-like antlers, sometimes with serpent legs, and surrounded by wildlife. The forest and woodlands were sacred to him, and the Celts feared them as places of power and danger. His ability to shift between human and animal form made him ruler of the animals, with the ability to summon them obediently at his call. Cernunnos was revered as a god whose power and favor could influence the Celts' survival—as lord of the forest, including trees and game, he controlled their major source of food and fuel. Certain gods from other cultures are thought to be derived from Cernunnos, and it is believed that his horns, as well as his association with death, inspired the contemporary image of Satan.

The Wee Folk and Fergus mac Leda

any Celtic legends involve races of fairies and elves that coexist with humans, secretly living underground or nocturnally. Many of the Wee Folk, as they are known, have lifestyles remarkably similar to that of humans, with royal scandals, war, and love coloring their fanciful lives.

Irish legends tell of a clan of elves with magical powers that dwelt in an overseas realm called Faylinn, the Land of the Wee Folk. In one incident, Iubdan, king of Faylinn, was presiding over a feast and liberally enjoying the free-flowing wine. He soon began boasting of his royal might and the invincible skill of his warriors—one in particular could even cut down a thistle with one blow. But the King's bard, Eisirt, countered with an account of a land called Ulster that was occupied by giants—greater warriors than even the Wee Folk. In anger, Iubdan ordered Eisirt to bring back evidence of these giants, upon threat of imprisonment.

Eisirt managed to reach Ulster and was taken to the palace of King Fergus mac Leda, where he was treated as an honored guest and feted with food and drink. Returning to Faylinn with Fergus' bard as proof, he told King Iubdan and his court of the wondrous sights he had seen. Eisirt then challenged the king to undertake the same quest and taste the giant king's porridge as he himself had just done. Under the code of chivalry, the reluctant Iubdan was compelled to go. Riding his fairy horse, Iubdan and his wife reached the gates of Fergus' palace in the dark of night. Fearful of the giants, they decided to secretly break into the palace, taste the porridge, and then leave. However, they were caught by a scullery maid and taken before Fergus, who received them hospitably but refused to let them go. To save their king, the Wee Folk came in great numbers to beg the release of Iubdan, but Fergus would only ransom the fairy king against the best of the Wee Folks' treasures—a pair of shoes which allowed its wearer to travel underwater as freely as on dry land. Exploring the depths of the lakes and rivers of Ireland soon became one of Fergus' chief pleasures, thanks to the magical gift from the fairies.